THE STEP BY STEP GUIDE ON HOW TO RETIRE RIGHT

The Step by Step Guide on How to Retire Right

**6 EASY TO FOLLOW STEPS TOWARDS CREATING
A SOUND RETIREMENT PLAN**

Bradley R. White, CFP®

© 2017 Bradley R. White, CFP®
All rights reserved.

ISBN-13: 9781974363858
ISBN-10: 1974363856

Table of Contents

Disclosure: vii

Introduction: ix

Chapter 1: Determine your monthly income goal, and at what age you want this to start (at what age you want to retire) 1

Chapter 2: Maximize income sources such as social security or pensions 9

Chapter 3: Develop income strategies for your investments to fund the gap between your total income goal and what the income sources bring in 20

Chapter 4: Develop an investment plan to address income needs, growth needs, liquidity needs, and stay within your risk tolerance 31

Chapter 5: Be Tax Efficient! With your Income Plan and Investment Plan 51

Chapter 6: Protect Your Retirement Income Plan Through a
Proper Health care coverage, Long Term Care, and Estate Plan · · · · · · 63

Chapter 7: Summary · 72

About the Author · 75

Disclosure:

This publication contains the opinions and ideas of its author. The strategies outlined in this book may not be suitable for every individual and are not guaranteed or warranted to produce any particular results.

Presentation of performance data herein does not imply that similar results will be achieved in the future. Any such data is provided merely for illustrative and discussion purposes; rather than focusing on the time periods used or the results derived. The reader should focus instead on the underlying principles. This book is sold with the understanding that neither publisher nor author, are providing legal, tax, investment, insurance, financial, accounting or other professional advice or services. If the reader requires such advice or services, a competent professional should be consulted. Relevant laws vary from state to state.

No warranty is made with respect to the accuracy or the completeness of the information contained herein. The author and publisher specifically disclaim any responsibility for any liability, loss, or risk, personal or otherwise, that is incurred as a consequence, directly or indirectly, by the use and application of any of the contents of this book.

The ideas expressed are not meant to be taken as advice to act upon.

You should find a trusted advisor to implement these ideas, if they are determined appropriate and suitable for your unique situation.

Insurance products and annuities are guaranteed by the insurance companies and the safety of these products are dependent on the claims paying ability of the insurance companies."

STEP BY STEP GUIDE ON HOW TO RETIRE RIGHT

INTRODUCTION:

Retirement is something you've never done before, it's inherently scary because of that fact alone. How can you know how to do something properly if you have no experience doing it whatsoever? Unlike other things, it isn't something you get to practice or gain experience in, you only get one shot to do it right.

Most people have no background in finance at all. You're not armed with the information to prepare a long term detailed cash flow forecast, to properly handle inflation, to navigate the tax code, or to research the best investment vehicles to support your plan.

Because of all of this it seems incredibly daunting and overwhelming to even begin and to actually get this done. This book was meant to give you the overall picture, followed by a step by step guide to build your retirement plan. We will cover all of the categories required when building a plan, and the individual steps to master each category.

I want you to always be very careful about general rules of thumb you hear about. As you will learn, everyone's situation is relatively similar. We all want to retire and live comfortably. We all have either a pension or social security, some savings and retirement accounts, we all invest, and we all pay taxes. However the nuances of each individual situation can create some shocking differences for why one strategy or investment is perfect for one person, and a horrible idea or investment for the next person. This is what creates the daunting and confusing challenge, and is what this book is meant to solve. This book is not going to give you specific recommendations, because I don't know your specific situation. This book will arm you with the things that need to be taken into consideration, and it will provide recommendations of what to do depending on your situation and what you are trying to accomplish.

Here is the step by step guide for how to build a proper retirement plan. Each of the subsequent chapters will be dedicated to mastering each step.

1) Determine your monthly income goal, and at what age you want this to start (at what age you want to retire).
2) Maximize income sources such as social security or pensions.
3) Develop income strategies for your investments to fund the gap between your total income goal and what income sources bring in.
4) Develop an investment plan to address income, growth, liquidity, and stay within your risk tolerance.
5) Be tax efficient! With the income and the investment plan.
6) Protect your plan through proper health care coverage, long term care, and estate planning.

CHAPTER 1

DETERMINE YOUR MONTHLY INCOME GOAL, AND AT WHAT AGE YOU WANT THIS TO START (AT WHAT AGE YOU WANT TO RETIRE)

It is impossible to choose the right social security strategy, the right investment, or to be tax efficient before you actually construct your retirement plan. Think about it, you don't start buying furniture or laying down carpet before you even finish the blue print of your home, do you? Therefore, the first thing I will teach you, is how a retirement plan is ACTUALLY constructed.

As you can see in the intro, the first step is to determine your monthly income goal, and at what age you want this to start (at what age you want to retire).

When addressing the income question, don't worry about things like inflation, taxes or mortgages being paid off just yet, we'll address those in a later chapter. Keep it very simple.

This is the first step in the process because it is what actually tells you if you have enough to retire or not.

In today's dollars, the way you currently WANT to live your life, how much do you need? Is that number $5,000 a month or $10,000 a month?

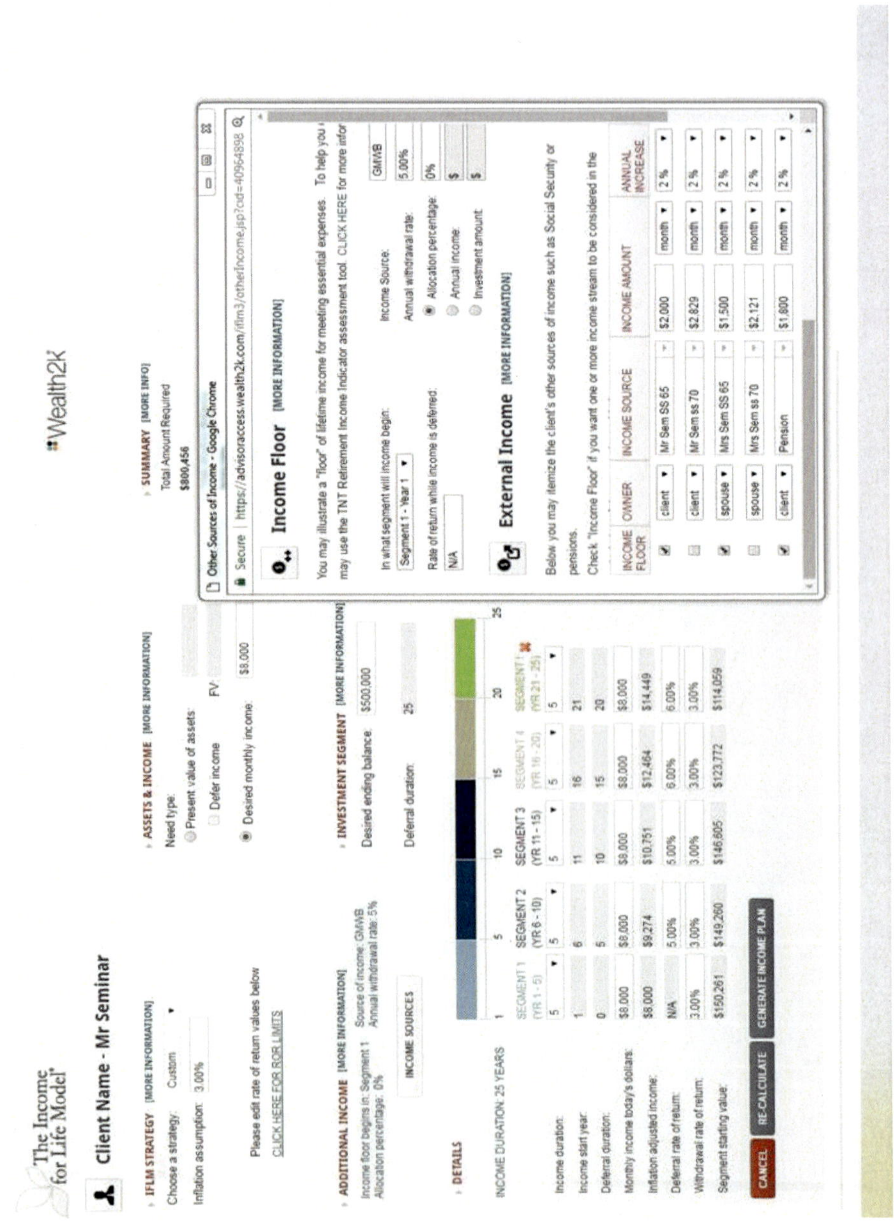

BRADLEY R. WHITE, CFP®

On the previous page is a chart with a 65 year old couple who want to determine if they can retire now. We built an income plan for $8,000 a month in gross dollars and appropriate tax assumptions for what they will net. From here, we make an inflation assumption of 3% per year, and a longevity assumption of running the plan until they are 90 years old, and include their comfort level of still having $500,000 in assets at that time. We make rate of return assumptions on their short term investments and long term investments, and we build in their pension and social security.

Once all of these assumptions are in, the software tells us they need $800,456 in total assets to run this plan. However, what if this couple was looking for $9,000 in gross dollars per month of income? You'll see on the next page a chart, with a goal of $9,000 a month. They now need to have saved $1,020,000.

BRADLEY R. WHITE, CFP®

The Income for Life Model®

Client Name - Mr Seminar

IFLM STRATEGY [MORE INFORMATION]
Choose a strategy: Custom
Inflation assumption: 3.00%

Please edit rate of return values below
CLICK HERE FOR ROR LIMITS

ASSETS & INCOME [MORE INFORMATION]
Need type:
☐ Present value of assets:
☐ Defer income   FV:
☑ Desired monthly income: $9,000

ADDITIONAL INCOME [MORE INFORMATION]
Income floor begins in: Segment 1   Source of income: GMWB
Allocation percentage: 0%   Annual withdrawal rate: 5%

INCOME SOURCES

INVESTMENT SEGMENT [MORE INFORMATION]
Desired ending balance: $500,000
Deferral duration: 25

	SEGMENT 1 (YR 1–5)	SEGMENT 2 (YR 6–10)	SEGMENT 3 (YR 11–15)	SEGMENT 4 (YR 16–20)	SEGMENT 5 (YR 21–25)
Income duration:	5	5	5	5	5
Income start year:	1	6	11	16	21
Deferral duration:	0	5	10	15	20
Monthly income today's dollars:	$9,000	$9,000	$9,000	$9,000	$9,000
Inflation adjusted income:	$9,000	$10,433	$12,095	$14,022	$16,255
Deferral rate of return:	N/A	5.00%	5.00%	6.00%	6.00%
Withdrawal rate of return:	3.00%	3.00%	3.00%	3.00%	3.00%
Segment starting value:	$205,914	$199,798	$192,524	$159,951	$145,398

CANCEL **RE-CALCULATE** **GENERATE INCOME PLAN**

> **DETAILS**
> INCOME DURATION: 25 YEARS

Wealth2k

SUMMARY [MORE INFO]
Total Amount Required
$1,020,084

Other Sources of Income - Google Chrome
Secure | https://advisoraccess.wealth2k.com/iflm3/otherIncome.jsp?cid=4096489...

Income Floor [MORE INFORMATION]
You may illustrate a "floor" of lifetime income for meeting essential expenses. To help you de may use the TNT Retirement Income Indicator assessment tool. CLICK HERE for more inform

In what segment will income begin: Income Source: GMWB
Segment 1 - Year 1   Annual withdrawal rate: 5.00%
Rate of return while income is deferred: ○ Allocation percentage: 0%
N/A   ● Annual income
                                     ○ Investment amount: $

External Income [MORE INFORMATION]
Below you may itemize the client's other sources of income such as Social Security or pensions.
Check "Income Floor" if you want one or more income stream to be considered in the

INCOME FLOOR	OWNER	INCOME SOURCE	INCOME AMOUNT		ANNUAL INCREASE	
☐	client	240k floor	$12,000	annual	0%
☐	client	300k 4% div int	$12,000	annual	1%
☑	client	Mr Sem SS 65	$2,000	month	2%
☑	client	Mr Sem ss 70	$2,829	month	2%
☑	spouse	Mrs Sem SS 65	$1,500	month	2%
☑	spouse	Mrs Sem ss 70	$2,121	month	2%
☐	client	Pension	$1,800	month	2%

This is why it's so crucial to understand your income goal before anything else. It would be pointless to worry about specific investments or tax strategies before constructing the blue print of the plan to ensure the numbers allow it to work in the first place. If this couple didn't save $800,456, they would need to lower their income goal, or delay retirement until the income goal was lowered to an amount they have actually accumulated in savings.

Once we have built this base plan with numbers that are actually feasible, we will go chapter by chapter to test the other assumptions such as the different ways to take social security, or different investment and tax strategies. If we can find solutions to keep the income the same but lower the amount needed, then we know we're choosing the correct vehicles given your specific situation.

The questions of how much income and when you want it to start, are the only two questions I can't answer for you. Once you have answered those questions, I (and any qualified retirement planner worth their salt) will be able to assist you with everything that you are about to learn in this book.

Even though I only give you those two responsibilities, I recognize that determining how much income you need is very difficult for a lot of people as they head into retirement. Retirement is the first time in your life you are deciding how much income to bring home each month. During your working years, our budgets and lifestyle needs develop organically over time based off what we're used to bringing home. Before you retire, it's incredibly important to figure out how much you are actually going to need.

How to Determine your Income Goal
(Note from author – if you already know your income goal you can skip to chapter 2)

Remember, I said you have to be careful about general rules of thumb floating around? Well here's the first example. A lot of you have heard, probably multiple times, that you'll need about 70% (or some percentage around there) of your pre-retirement income once you retire. Having walked several hundred people through retirement, I honestly have no idea where people are getting that from. I have yet to find a person who has told me they want to do less in retirement. Every day is Saturday now, this is the culmination of all of those years of hard work and ideally time to enjoy yourself. There are two different ways to figure this out.

1) The Simple Way

Start by taking a look at the total net income of your household before retirement. When it comes to work income, do not use your actual salary as a relevant number. You pay federal, state, local, and payroll taxes, you might have 401k contributions, medical and dental expenses, and other things that get deducted before you get your net income. If you get paid twice a month, simply look at your bank account and see what amount ACTUALLY made its way to your bank. Of course include everyone contributing to the household.

Note – if you are on bi-weekly pay, then take this number and multiple by 26 and then divide by 12 to get your average monthly net income.

If this is your households only source of income, then great! Your exercise stops here. However, if you have rental income or other forms of income you are currently receiving, please add these net amounts as well.

THIS is the amount of your monthly income. For most people, this is a great starting point towards your income goal in retirement. Essentially, you're just replicating your current income in retirement and continuing to live your same lifestyle.

You might, however, be saving money each month while working. In retirement, and this is an important point, you don't want to SAVE money any longer, you just simply take less out of the accounts.

Example: if your household's net income before retirement was $10,000 a month, but you found yourself saving $2,000 a month on average into your checking account, then your income need in retirement should be $8,000 a month. This would be the number we will use to build your retirement plan.

2) Detailed Budget

Don't get me wrong, even if the simple version above gave you the answers you needed and you are living within your means, it's a good idea to do a detailed budget.

Now it's time to start looking at your current expenses. I recommend first segregating all of your essential expenses and discretionary expenses. Essential expenses are things like housing, transportation, food, medical, etc. Discretionary expenses are all of the wants you have such as vacations, going out to eat and your hobbies.

Note, if you have a fixed mortgage the good news is that your income will go up over time because of inflation, which means the cost of housing will become a smaller and smaller part of your overall budget.

You then want to take a look at any expenses you currently have that will disappear in the future. Let's say a part of your budget today is your mortgage of $2,000 a month and is scheduled to be paid off in 10 more years. This means you want to build into your retirement plan this expense dropping off in ten years. Please note, if you wrap in property taxes and insurance into the mortgage payment, those expenses will continue even after you pay off your mortgage. Only drop the principal and interest part of the payment.

Other examples could be things such as kids that are still living with you or their education expenses.

It's also important to take into consideration expenses that aren't there currently but that could be there in the future. These could include new car purchases and payments, weddings, house repairs or construction, and medical costs.

Please be conservative when doing your budget. If you think you spend between $400 - $600 a month on food, then put down $600. Once we finish constructing a retirement plan, if we find out there is a shortfall, then it will be time to go back to the budget and start making some concessions. When putting the budget together initially however, be honest with yourself and conservative with projections.

Once you finish adding all of your essential and discretionary expenses, I recommend adding one final column for the random or unforeseen expenses that come up throughout the year. I have a column in my personal budget simply titled "life," because life always seems to come up unexpectedly.

Adding up all of your "need" and "want" expenses will determine your income goal.

You have now determined your income goal in retirement, and it's time for all of the other dominos to start falling!

CHAPTER 2

Maximize income sources such as social security or pensions

You will have some income coming your way in retirement. For most of us this will include social security. For others, it may also include a pension, rental income, or other forms of passive income as well. Before you do anything else, it is incredibly important to maximize these sources. Making poor decisions can mean tens of thousands of dollars or more in a retirement plan, it's important to choose them wisely.

Social Security:

In order to choose social security benefits correctly, you have to look at it in two ways. First, you need to understand all of the complicated rules, options, and strategies of the system itself in order to take advantage of it to your highest capability. Second, you need to then organize those options within the context of the other things going on with your retirement plan.

I could write an entire book about social security itself. This excerpt is meant to cover all of the major things to consider when choosing social security benefits. It is not meant to cover some of the detailed parts of the code, and I strongly suggest you seek out an expert to personally help you choose your social security benefits.

You can start receiving your benefits as early as age 62, and as late as age 70. However, social security gives you a "Full Retirement Age" which is based upon your year of birth. See the chart on the next page to determine your FRA.

Social Security Eligibility and Benefits

Year of birth[a]	Full (normal) Retirement Age	Months between age 62 and full retirement age[b]	At Age 62[c]			
			A $1000 retirement benefit would be reduced to	The retirement benefit is reduced by[d]	A $500 spouse's benefit would be reduced to	The spouse benefit is reduced by[e]
1937 or earlier	65	36	$800	20%	$375	25.00%
1938	65 and 2 months	38	$791	20.83%	$370	25.83%
1939	65 and 4 months	40	$783	21.67%	$366	26.67%
1940	65 and 6 months	42	$775	22.5%	$362	27.50%
1941	65 and 8 months	44	$766	23.33%	$358	28.33%
1942	65 and 10 months	46	$758	24.17%	$354	29.17%
1943-1954	66	48	$750	25.00%	$350	30.00%
1955	66 and 2 months	50	$741	25.83%	$345	30.83%
1956	66 and 4 months	52	$733	26.67%	$341	31.67%
1957	66 and 6 months	54	$725	27.50%	$337	32.50%
1958	66 and 8 months	56	$716	28.33%	$333	33.33%
1959	66 and 10 months	58	$708	29.17%	$329	34.17%
1960 and later	67	60	$700	30.00%	$325	35.00%

[a] If you are born on January 1, use the prior year of birth.
[b] Applies only if you are born on the 2nd of the month; otherwise the number of reduction months is one less than the number shown.
[c] Reduction applied to primary insurance amount ($1,000 in this example). The percentage reduction is 5/9 of 1% per month for the first 36 months and 5/12 of 1% for each additional month.
[d] Reduction applied to $500, which is 50% of the primary insurance amount in this example. The percentage reduction is 25/36 of 1% per month for the first 36 months and 5/12 of 1% for each additional month.

Source: http://www.socialsecurity.gov/OACT/quickcalc/earlyretire.html accessed August 8, 2015

The FRA chart is the only true social security number we all have. The social security administration simply penalize your benefit down to age 62 if you take your benefit early or increase your benefit up to age 70 for delaying retirement benefits. Your full retirement age is an incredibly important number for social security. Every rule and strategy for social security is different between 62 and your FRA, and those same rules or strategies are different between your FRA and 70.

First, how much will social security grow for you if you do not take it at 62? From 62 until your FRA, your benefit grows by five ninths of a percent every month. This is the same thing as saying 6 2/3% every year. However, from FRA until age 70 it will grow by 8% simple interest each year.

This begs the single most popular question I get regarding social security. "Brad, I get a much bigger paycheck at 70 than I do at age 62, but that's eight years of a paycheck I could have been getting immediately. Therefore, if I do wait until 70, how long do I need to live to catch up and break even with those immediate missed payments?"

The social security administration has a very complex rule called AIME (average indexed monthly earnings) that essentially gives everyone a break-even point around age 80. Based off of some small factors it could be age 78 for some, or 81 for others, but we'll just use age 80 for our discussion. This means if you wait until age 70 to take your social security, every year you live past the age of 80 you will get more social security dollars over your lifetime because you waited to take your benefit. This is 100% true for everyone. Therefore, if I think I'm going to live past the age 80, wouldn't I just want to wait to take social security until I'm 70? The answer is, not necessarily.

Let's say you want to retire at age 62 and you needed $8,000 a month with which to live. If you take your reduced age 62 social security, you wouldn't have to pull as much money from your investments to get to your total goal of $8,000. If you chose not to take social security and wait until age 70, then from 62 to 70 you will be drawing your income exclusively from your portfolio, and your portfolio will be lower forever after because of this. If you wait until age 70 to collect social security, and live past the age of 80, you will get more social security income over your life – that's true. However, the reduction in investment returns over your life by draining your accounts down more rapidly can actually outweigh that fact and cause it to still be a bad idea! In other words, how you take social security is not just a factor of how long you will live. Take a look at "Breakeven Analysis" on the next page.

Breakeven Analysis Comparing Two Strategies:

Year	Mr	Mrs	Mr (PIA=2143.0)	Mrs (PIA=1607.0)	Annual Benefits	Cumulative Benefits	Mr (PIA=2143.0)	Mrs (PIA=1607.0)	Annual Benefits	Cumulative Benefits	Difference
				Both take at 65				Delayed			
2017	65	65	$2,000	$1,500	$27,999	$27,999	$0	$0	$0	$0	($27,999)
2018	66	66	$2,040	$1,530	$42,838	$70,837	$0	$0	$0	$0	($70,837)
2019	67	67	$2,081	$1,560	$43,693	$114,530	$0	$0	$0	$0	($114,530)
2020	68	68	$2,122	$1,592	$44,567	$159,097	$0	$0	$0	$0	($159,097)
2021	69	69	$2,165	$1,623	$45,456	$204,553	$0	$0	$0	$0	($204,553)
2022	70	70	$2,208	$1,656	$46,363	$250,916	$0	$2,342	$43,714	$43,714	($207,202)
2023	71	71	$2,252	$1,689	$47,290	$298,206	$3,123	$2,388	$66,882	$110,596	($187,610)
2024	72	72	$2,297	$1,722	$48,234	$346,440	$3,185	$2,436	$68,216	$178,813	($167,627)
2025	73	73	$2,343	$1,757	$49,199	$395,638	$3,249	$2,485	$69,581	$248,394	($147,244)
2026	74	74	$2,390	$1,792	$50,182	$445,820	$3,314	$2,534	$70,972	$319,365	($126,455)
2027	75	75	$2,438	$1,828	$51,185	$497,005	$3,380	$2,585	$72,390	$391,755	($105,250)
2028	76	76	$2,486	$1,864	$52,208	$549,213	$3,448	$2,637	$73,837	$465,592	($83,621)
2029	77	77	$2,536	$1,902	$53,250	$602,463	$3,516	$2,689	$75,312	$540,904	($61,559)
2030	78	78	$2,587	$1,940	$54,314	$656,777	$3,587	$2,743	$76,816	$617,720	($39,057)
2031	79	79	$2,638	$1,978	$55,399	$712,177	$3,658	$2,798	$78,352	$696,072	($16,105)
						Break Even Point					
2032	80	80	$2,691	$2,018	$56,506	$768,682	$3,732	$2,854	$79,916	$775,988	$7,306
2033	81	81	$2,745	$2,058	$57,635	$826,317	$3,806	$2,911	$81,514	$857,501	$31,184
2034	82	82	$2,800	$2,099	$58,788	$885,105	$3,882	$2,969	$83,143	$940,645	$55,540
2035	83	83	$2,856	$2,141	$59,962	$945,067	$3,960	$3,028	$84,804	$1,025,449	$80,382
2036	84	84	$2,913	$2,184	$61,159	$1,006,226	$4,039	$3,089	$86,496	$1,111,945	$105,719
2037	85	85	$2,971	$2,227	$62,380	$1,068,605	$4,119	$3,150	$88,225	$1,200,170	$131,565
2038	86	86	$3,030	$2,272	$63,628	$1,132,233	$4,202	$3,213	$89,987	$1,290,157	$157,924
2039	87	87	$3,091	$2,317	$64,898	$1,197,131	$4,286	$3,277	$91,786	$1,381,942	$184,811
2040	88	88	$3,153	$2,364	$66,196	$1,263,327	$4,371	$3,343	$93,620	$1,475,563	$212,236
2041	89	89	$3,216	$2,411	$67,518	$1,330,845	$4,459	$3,410	$95,490	$1,571,053	$240,208
2042	90	90	$3,280	$2,459	$22,956	$1,353,801	$4,548	$3,478	$32,466	$1,603,519	$249,718

14

Remember, the same 65 year old couple with the $8,000 a month income goal from the first example? See the chart again on the next page. As you can see, if they wait until age 70 and both live until 90, they will get an additional $249,718 dollars combined in social security benefits. However, take a look at what happens to their retirement plan once we assume they wait to take social security. When we assumed they took their social securities at age 65 they needed $800,456 in savings.

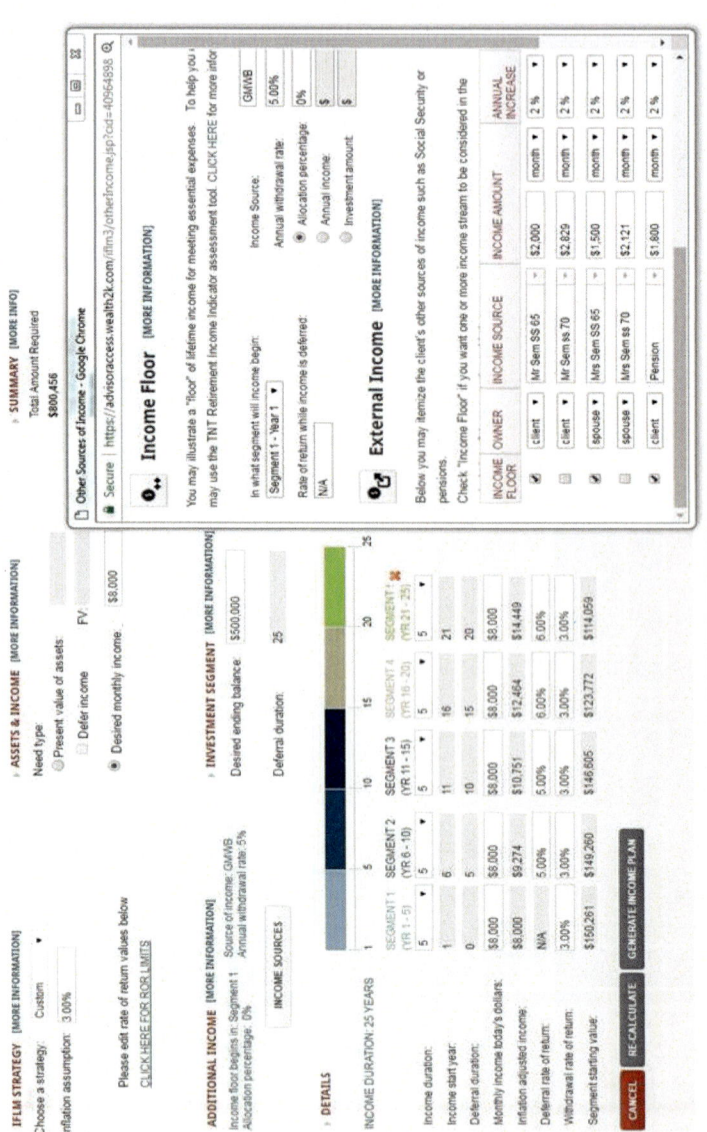

Leaving everything else the same and making this one change means now they need $850,846. In other words, when looking at social security only, it suggested they would benefit by almost $250,000 dollars. However, in reality it's a $50,000 mistake for them to wait to take social security given the nuances of their specific situation.

You need to consider the age in which you want to retire, your overall income goal, the size of your retirement savings, and tax considerations. For some of us those factors will tell us to wait as long as possible to take social security, and for others it will suggest that it's a good idea to take social security early.

Spousal Rights:

If you are married for at least one year, or you were married for at least ten years but are now divorced, you need to be aware of spousal rights that exist within the system.

A spousal benefit means you, at your own FRA, can collect 50% of your spouse's FRA amount if it's greater than your own. If you and your spouse both reached your FRA's, their benefit was $2,000 a month at that age and yours was only $500 a month at that age; you would be entitled to a $1,000 check as a spouse. You would not get BOTH benefits, just $1,000 total. It will not harm your spouse's benefit at all, they will still receive their full $2,000 per month. Even if you had no benefit whatsoever, you would still be entitled to the $1,000 a month spousal right. If you try to collect your spousal right at your age 62 however, you would only be entitled to 36% of your spouse's FRA amount. Each month that 36% climbs slowly until it reaches the full 50% level at your FRA where it is maximized. Another important point to remember is that your percentage as a spouse is ALWAYS based off of your spouse's FRA amount regardless of when they take their benefit.

Example: You and your spouse are both age 62. You have no social security benefit because you didn't work, and your spouse's FRA benefit is $2,000 a month. Your spouse decides to take early at their age 62, and therefore doesn't get to collect $2,000 a month but instead gets $1,500. You then decide to claim your spousal benefit. First, is that your percentage is reduced to 36% because of YOUR age of when you filed. However, even though your spouse filed for their age 62 benefit, you will still get a 720 dollar spousal check (36% of the $2,000 FRA amount). It does not matter at all when your spouse files for their benefits, your percentage is always based off of their FRA benefit. In this example, the spouse is getting punished for taking their benefit early which is why they only receive $1500. You are also getting punished by taking your spousal benefit early because your percentage is only 36%, but please don't assume you get 36% of the reduced $1,500 as this is one of the hardest things to remember.

Two final points about spousal rights: the first, is that a spouse does not have the ability to file a spousal benefit if the other spouse hasn't filed for their own benefit. The second, is that a spousal benefit never gets better than the 50% level at the spouses FRA. Our own social security will continue to grow until age 70 if we want it to, but for a spouse it will never get better than the 50% level at their FRA.

Again, this book is meant to cover the main considerations for social security. We have not even begun to talk about switching techniques, survivor rights, children's benefits, Windfall Elimination Provision and Government Pension Offset, to name a few. Please seek an expert when choosing your own benefits.

A Quick Note about Pensions:

If you are fortunate enough to have a pension, then congratulations, as they are becoming extinct for the rest of us. Once again, pensions are something very specific to each company, so I won't be going into tremendous detail on how to choose yours in this book. Essentially, you need to go through a similar exercise and toggle back and forth the lump sum option for which you are eligible, and compare it with the income options offered you. The items of consideration for your pension choice are as follows:

1) Is the income a good deal compared to the size of the lump sum they're offering you?
2) What is your total income need, and how much is covered already from social security or other sources of income?
3) What is the size of other savings you have should you choose not to take the lump sum?
4) Do you have legacy goals for the money?
5) What is the long term health viability of the company promising the pension? Do you have any health conditions altering your normal life expectancy?
6) What is your tax situation now and your RMD situation once you reach 70 1/2?

Each of these items needs to be looked at through the lens of your specific plan to determine the optimal way for you to choose your pension.

CHAPTER 3

DEVELOP INCOME STRATEGIES FOR YOUR INVESTMENTS TO FUND THE GAP BETWEEN YOUR TOTAL INCOME GOAL AND WHAT THE INCOME SOURCES BRING IN

For most of us, the total income goal is not going to be covered by our income sources alone. We're going to need our retirement savings to generate the rest of the income we need, or "fund the gap." If I'm looking for $8,000 a month as an example and my income sources provide me $6,000 a month, then my gap is $2,000 and that is what my investments need to generate.

The most important thing to understand is the concept of the withdrawal rate of your money. Back in 1992, a very famous financial planner named William Bengen ran a comprehensive and detailed study, which yielded him the Nobel Prize. The study was based off of the question "how much money can I pull out of my retirement savings without running out of money someday?" Mr. Bengen then started to look at every possible rolling 30 year period from the great depression on with a 60% stock 40% bond allocation. His study showed that if you pulled out 4% of your portfolio each year, you would not run out of money over the 30 years in 100% of the scenarios. Therefore, this 4% withdrawal rate became a rule of thumb for retirees to follow. However, in 1992 the ten year U.S Treasury note was paying around 7.5% which is drastically higher than we see as of the writing of this book in 2017. Also, we're living longer today than we were back then. This has prompted a lot of institutions to go back and look at Mr. Bengen's study and test it under today's conditions. What they have discovered is that a 3% withdrawal rate is now the prudent rule of thumb to follow in order to still achieve a 100% success rate for a 30 year timeframe.

This may not seem like a big difference at first, I mean what's 1% between friends, right? Well let's take a look at the glaring visual below.

Withdrawal rate

40,000 a year is the income goal.

If I could get a 4% withdrawal rate, I need 1,000,000.

If I could only get a 3% withdrawal rate, I would need *1,333,333 dollars.*

I would need to grow my money by 33% to get the same income, as a 1% extra withdrawal rate.

This visual is usually a shocking wakeup call of how important the withdrawal rate number really is. Interest rates are so low, we can't just park our money in CD's and Bonds to give us enough of a withdrawal rate. Also taking into consideration how long we're now living, we need to develop income strategies to help boost our chances of long term success. There are three main strategies to look at today: Flooring, dividend and interest, and laddering.

Flooring:

This is a strategy where you take a PORTION of your overall assets and use them to fund an investment designed to deliver a high degree of guaranteed consistent monthly income. Let's say you were again looking for $8,000 a month of total income, where $7,000 of that amount is essential and the final $1,000 is the discretionary part. Both spouses have combined social security and pension income of $6,000 per month, and therefore the gap to cover the essential expenses is still $1,000 per month, and the total gap is $2,000 per month.

With a flooring methodology, you would first want to find out how to guarantee $1,000 per month of income so that you know at least your essential expenses are covered for life no matter what happens with the markets over time.

Let's say you could find an example of an investment that would pay a 5% withdrawal rate guaranteed for life for a 65 year old. This means you would have to place $240,000 into this investment to guarantee another 1,000 dollar a month paycheck ($240,000 multiplied by 5% is $12,000 per year or $1,000 per month).

Positives of the Flooring Strategy:

First, is the guaranteed nature of the income. It is comforting in retirement to know that if all else fails you have your essential expenses covered for life.

Second, is the high withdrawal percentage typically associated with this strategy. Remember, our withdrawal strategy example from earlier on how valuable the 4% withdrawal rate was compared to the 3%? With the flooring strategy if you can guarantee such a high withdrawal rate for income from just part of your assets, you preserve more of the remaining assets to simply keep growing for you.

Third is the simplistic nature of the strategy. There is no ongoing maintenance with this strategy as it's simply a guaranteed income stream you set in motion.

Negatives of the Flooring Strategy:

Depending on how big your income gap is, you might have to use more of your assets to fund this strategy than you are comfortable doing, leaving you only a small portion of assets remaining outside of this strategy.

Lack of inflation control is another potential downfall. Your income gap may be $1,000 on day one of retirement, but because of inflation you need to increase your income each year in retirement. If you purchase an investment where the $1,000 income stream stays flat for life, we need to address where the additional income is coming from as the years go on.

Note – there are investments that guarantee an inflation protected income stream.

Summary for Flooring:

If you are someone who is more risk averse and simply looking for an income stream, then as long as you build in other accounts that can grow for inflation, a flooring strategy for part of your assets is a very viable option. If you are someone that likes constant flexibility with your investments and doesn't mind risk and volatility, this tends not to be a strategy for you.

Dividend and Interest:

This is the traditional form of income planning for retirees. The idea would be to place your money into investments that generate a consistent amount of dividends and/or interest. You simply collect those dividends and/or interest to fund your income gap, while leaving the principal of the investment alone.

As an example, let's say I purchased $100,000 worth of ten year Coca Cola 5% bonds. This means I lent Coca Cola $100,000 for ten years, and in exchange I will get $5,000 of interest income. At the end of the ten years I get my $100,000 returned to me. Because the bond is simply a loan, as long as I buy it from a very stable company then it is considered a relatively safe way to get the income I need to fund my gap, without reducing my principal over the 10 years.

I could also decide to purchase $100,000 worth of Coca Cola stock that pays a 4% dividend yield. By purchasing stock I am now a part owner in Coca Cola, which means there is risk I could lose money if the company isn't as profitable as we hope, or I can make a lot of money if it ends up being much more profitable then we think. However, regardless of what's happening with the price of the stock itself, the goal is that the dividend will come in regardless.

Let's say hypothetically Coca Cola stock was worth $100 per share, and paying $4 worth of dividends per year for each share you own. This would equal the 4% dividend yield (4 divided into the $100 share price). Let's then say some bad news came out about Coca Cola and the stock fell to $90 per share. The goal is that coca cola would still pay you $4 worth of dividends for each share you own. The difference is that now the yield would have moved up to 4.44% (4 divided into the $90 share price).

The ideology of dividend stocks is that if you choose companies you feel are going to be able to consistently pay the dividend for years to come, you don't have to worry about the stock price in the short term. You can simply collect the consistent dividends for cash flow. Ideally your principal is also growing over time because on top of the dividends you receive, you're hoping the price of the stock is increasing over time as well.

Positives of the Dividend and Interest Strategy:

First, this can be a viable strategy to generate income and not reduce your principal, which is a very comfortable feeling for retirees. Knowing you can get the consistent income you're looking for without having to dip into your nest egg is of course a way to prevent from ever running out of money.

Second, if you are choosing historically safe and stable investments, then it is also a very easy strategy to follow without much short term maintenance or changes needed.

Negatives of the Dividend and Interest Strategy:

By far the biggest challenge of this strategy today is the historically low interest rate environment. Let's look back at the example we gave in the flooring section. This couple is looking for an additional $1,000 per month to fund their essential income gap.

Back in 1992 the 10 year treasury was at 7.5%. If I wanted to purchase something safe to fund my $1,000 income gap, I would have only had to invest $160,000. If the 10 year treasury was currently at 2.5%, then I would have to put in $480,000 to get the same results today.

Low interest rates have also caused investors to take more risk than they would otherwise historically as they chase a higher yield. As an example, a risky stock may have a 7% yield and therefore an investor chooses this over Coca Cola, however the company then eventually goes bankrupt and you lose your entire principal for simply trying to chase a larger dividend.

Summary for the Dividend and Interest Strategy:

Bottom line is in a low interest rate environment this is going to be harder to employ. However, if the size of your assets are relatively large compared to the income gap, a diversified portfolio of many stocks and bonds, even at a low yield, might still be able to get the job done.

If you are someone that wants to see the principal of your accounts stay the same or even grow while you collect income, and you don't mind the fluctuating value of your accounts as the stock values go up and down, this strategy can be very attractive when using a proper diversified approach. If you are someone who would prefer a higher degree of dependable income and doesn't mind if principal goes down over time, and if you are risk averse and don't enjoy seeing fluctuating values of your accounts, this strategy tends to not be for you.

Laddering Strategy:

This is a strategy that looks at your income needs and investments in a time sequence. It is a strategy that has gained popularity in the recent decade because low rates have hurt the viability of the dividend and interest strategy mentioned above.

We typically create a short term bucket of investments designed to fund the income gap for the first few years of retirement. You will spend down this short term bucket, however at the same time you have other investments designed to simply grow in your mid term and long term buckets.

THE STEP BY STEP GUIDE ON HOW TO RETIRE RIGHT

Looking back at the example from chapter one, and the chart on the previous page, you will see we have actually already done this. Of the $800,456 needed total, we know to fund the income gap with a laddered strategy. It's going to take $150,261 to cover the first 5 years. It will then take $149,260 to cover years 6-10, etc.

Positives of the Laddered Strategy:

The main point with this strategy is to help you choose the proper investments for your plan. If you can understand where your income is coming from you can invest those dollars in something safe and liquid. In today's world you won't get a great rate of return, but you also won't need to because you've built this into your plan and you know the numbers work.

It's also important to understand where your long term growth accounts are. When you retire, not all of your money retires at the same time. If you look at segment 5 you will see there is $114,059 that we won't need for 20 years. This means we can still invest aggressively into long term stocks with this money, and if the market goes down initially, we have 20 years to recover and more than likely achieve better rates of return because of it.

Negatives with this Strategy:

The biggest negative is there can be more maintenance involved. As an example, you may have earmarked an account to be short term and another to be long term. However, if the markets move unexpectedly, it may make sense to change your investment strategy accordingly and have to adjust this plan many times along the way.

Also, your risk tolerance on the long-term accounts can come into question. Even though we identify money you won't need for 20 years, as an example, when the bad markets occur it can cause some investors to panic and sell regardless of how it was built into the plan.

A Combination of Strategies:

As you can see each strategy has components it does well, and other areas where it is deficient. Your overall income needs, the size of your income gap, the size of your assets overall, your risk tolerances, all should dictate your approach. Please keep in mind, it could very likely be a combination of the above strategies.

Example: 65 year old couple with an $8,000 total income need. $7,000 is the essential need and $1,000 is the discretionary. They have a combined $6,000 a month from their social securities and pensions. They have $800,000 in total assets.

This 65 year old couple may decide to first reduce their risk and cover their essential expenses by taking $240,000 of their assets to fund the flooring strategy and create $1,000 per month.

Next, they might build a well-diversified historically stable portfolio of different stocks and bonds to create a blended yield of 4%. This means they have to place $300,000 of their assets into this investment which will yield them an additional $1,000 per month to cover their discretionary expenses and the rest of their income gap.

Now with $540,000 of their $800,000 in assets, they have covered their entire gap and achieved $8,000 a month of total income. The flooring method is guaranteed, but lacks flexibility and inflation control. The bond income from the portfolio is safe and stable without reducing principal, but most likely a low yield in today's environment. The stock dividend yield is high and stable, and can grow to help with inflation, but is riskier than the flooring or bond income. The combination, however, is meant to cover all of those planning needs.

Finally, the remaining $260,000 is invested in a laddered approach. Life will happen along the way which means you will need to grab a lump sum in addition to the $8,000 of regular monthly income. You will now have a short term bucket to grab this money from in the future. Also, to combat inflation and keep your principal intact or growing, you will have created a long term bucket that you won't need for many years and invested accordingly.

You now have a solid income strategy!

CHAPTER 4
DEVELOP AN INVESTMENT PLAN TO ADDRESS INCOME NEEDS, GROWTH NEEDS, LIQUIDITY NEEDS, AND STAY WITHIN YOUR RISK TOLERANCE

Everyone would love to know what the stock market is going to do tomorrow or what the next breakout investment is going to be. The problem is no one, and I mean no one, has any clue what's going to happen next. The goal of this chapter is not to tell you what stock to buy next, but what the underlying important principles are to investing within the context of a retirement income plan. We will then talk about two categories of investment choices – mutual funds and annuities.

One of the most common investment mistakes people make is choosing an investment because they like the way it sounds without regard for what they actually NEED this particular part of their money to do for them. This is why we covered the income strategy chapter first. If you are following my steps to build a retirement plan, and conclude that you need this particular part of your money to fund a flooring strategy, then you shouldn't be looking at stocks. On the other hand, if this part of your money is meant to fund the long term aggressive bucket of your plan, then stocks are perfectly appropriate and you shouldn't be looking at short term safe bonds. That is just one of many examples.

Another major hurdle for the average investor is coming to grips with the fact there is no such thing as the perfect investment. There is a universe of different investment options and hundreds of versions of each choice.

Because of this, I think it's important to simplify things into the three characteristics that all of us are looking for with every investment.

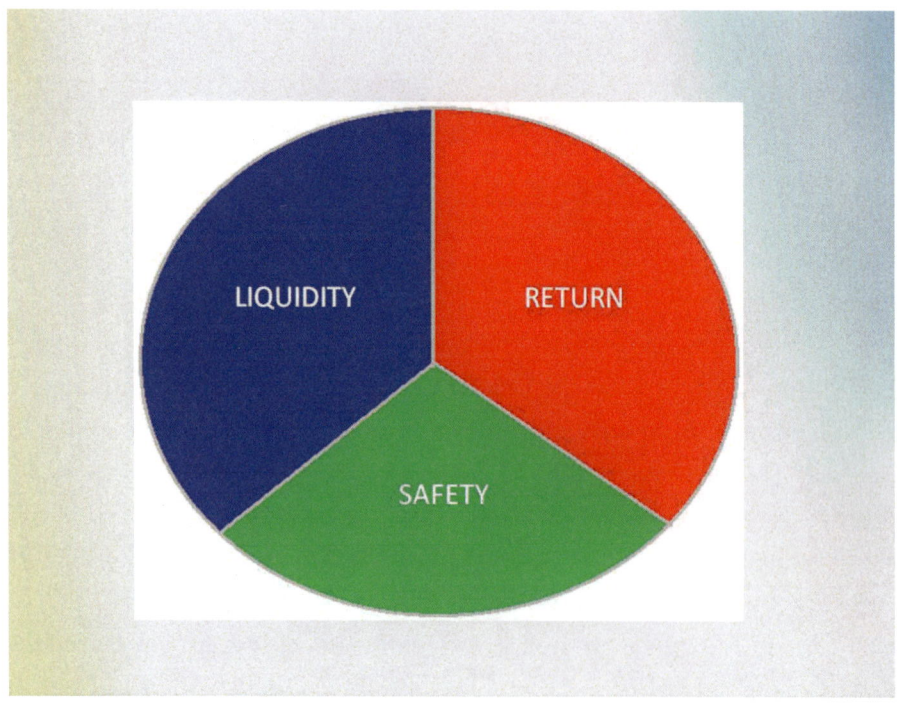

If we could find an investment that was safe, was liquid if we needed our money back in a pinch, and gave us the return we were looking for then investment advisors would all be out of a job, and we would all put our money there. The problem is that no investment will do all three of these things well at the same time. Investments tend to do two of the three things well at any one time. We have to decide what to prioritize and what we're willing to give up.

If we keep money in the bank it will be safe and liquid, but in today's low interest rate environment we get little return. The stock market is liquid and over long periods of time has delivered solid returns, but we certainly throw safety out of the window at least in the short term. We also go into investments designed to be safe and give a better rate of return. If we choose that world, we must give up some liquidity. This is why banks pay more for a five year CD than they do for a 6 month CD. We simply traded liquidity to get a safe return.

We also want to look at investments as achieving one of three basic goals.

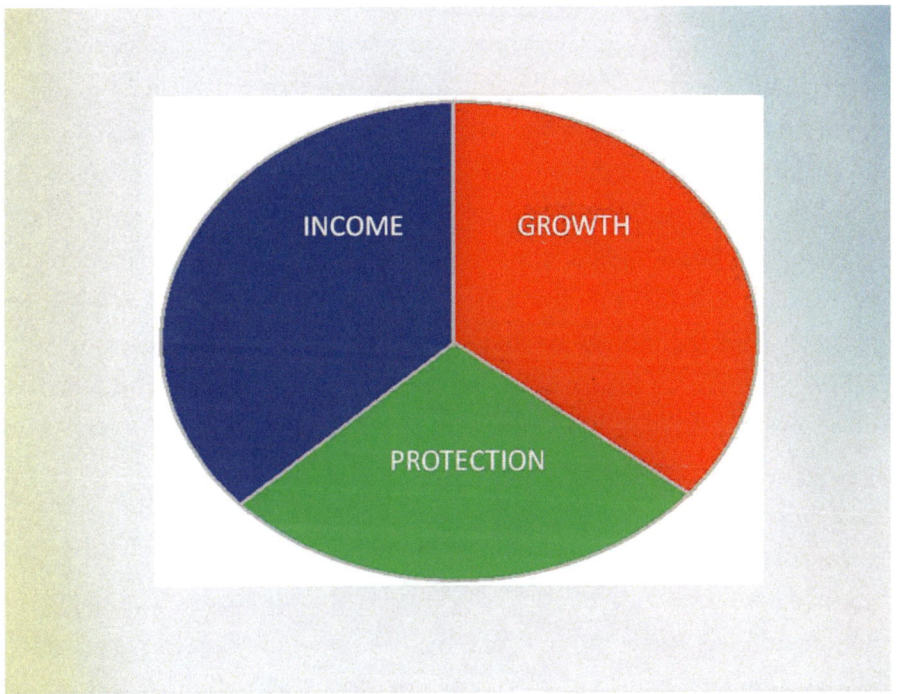

Investments that do a great job of delivering consistent income typically don't also do a great job of growth, and vice versa. So once again, we first build out our income plan, understanding our income needs and what kind of a gap we need to fund, and then choose the income strategies with which we feel most comfortable. We will then understand how much of the above goals we are shooting for, and be able to choose the appropriate investments accordingly.

As human beings, we have a natural tendency to immediately point out the flaw in something. In a world where the stock market has risen to all-time highs and interest rates to all-time lows, I have seen a tremendous amount of people who feel they are in investment purgatory and don't seem to like any of the options out there.

This is where diversification becomes so paramount. Let's say you have already built an income plan that will achieve the income gap and fund it through flooring and dividend and interest strategies. You are now wondering how to invest the remaining monies you have. We can then look at a laddered approach. We know how much of your money is needed for the short term bucket, and we find an investment that is safe and liquid. We build into the plan the low rate of return it will achieve, and the plan works great. Now you know how much of your money should be in an investment that is safe and liquid.

We then take a look at the longer term buckets of your plan, and realize we need to achieve a certain rate of return to make this plan work, and we don't need the money for many years. This is where you choose how to achieve that rate of return. Do you want the money liquid and you don't mind taking risk, such as the stock market? Or potentially are you someone who doesn't like taking risk, even with your long term money? Here you can find an investment that is safer and will give you the return you need, however, it won't be liquid for a period of time. The beauty here is you already have a short term liquid bucket for when you need money, so you can go find an illiquid investment and not have the risk for when a liquidity need arises.

In summary, you follow the first few steps to build a plan and understand your income and growth needs. Then you can diversify into a few different key investment strategies where the combination of them will help keep your overall money safe, liquid, and getting the rate of return needed to run your plan. The key is to understand what you need your money to do and search for the likeminded investment, and place the appropriate dollar amount there. Then, whatever the investment lacks, simply compliment it with a different investment that specializes in that characteristic, and do this once again with the third investment achieving the third characteristic. The right combination can give you everything you need.

Risk Tolerance:

The next step, after assessing what you need from your investments, is to understand who you are as an investor and stay consistent and in your comfort zone.

Let's say you had to go from San Diego to New York, and I offered you two different ways to get there. The first is a military Jet going 800 mph doing flips and spins. The second, is a nice plushy first class seat on a 747 with zero turbulence whatsoever – plus a nice hot towel. Which would you choose? Me personally? I would choose the first class seat. I flat out couldn't handle that wild ride, even if I got to my final destination an hour or two earlier. The risk just wasn't worth the reward for me. I know, with confidence, I'll make it to my destination and I'll enjoy the ride. With the jet I fear I could crash, and even if it makes it successfully, I might have a heart attack along the way.

This may not be a perfect analogy, but you can probably draw the comparisons to investing conservatively vs. aggressively. Over long periods of time the stock market has always proven to get to its final destination, but there will inevitably be some gut crunching moments along the way. For a retiree, you need to stop and think about your ability to handle a 20% drop, 30% drop, or even more with the rest of your life money now that you don't have the time or ability to make it back. I also suggest you apply real dollars instead of percentages. If you have one million dollars, don't say a 30% decline to yourself, ask yourself what you will want to do when your account is down 300,000 dollars! If the answer is that you just couldn't take it anymore and you would want out of the market, then you shouldn't invest that way in the first place.

After the market has a sell off this is logically the best time to try and buy stocks. After the market has had a huge run up, this is logically the last time to buy stocks. However, every study of investor behavior and fund flows shows the exact opposite.

Dalbar conducts a study each year and this is just small part of their findings in their 2016 study.

	Investor Returns[1]					Barclays Aggregate Bond Index
	Equity Funds	Asset Allocation Funds	Fixed Income Funds	Inflation	S&P 500	
30 Year	3.66	1.65	0.59	2.60	10.35	6.73
20 Year	4.67	2.11	0.51	2.20	8.19	5.34
10 Year	4.23	1.89	0.39	1.88	7.31	4.51
5 Year	6.92	3.28	0.10	1.58	12.57	3.25
3 Year	8.85	3.81	-1.76	1.07	15.13	1.44
12 Months	-2.28	-3.48	-3.11	0.95	1.38	0.55

[1]. **Returns are for the period ending December 31, 2015.** *Average equity investor, average bond investor and average asset allocation investor performance results are calculated using data supplied by the Investment Company Institute. Investor returns are represented by the change in total mutual fund assets after excluding sales, redemptions and exchanges. This method of calculation captures realized and unrealized capital gains, dividends, interest, trading costs, sales charges, fees, expenses and any other costs. After calculating investor returns in dollar terms, two percentages are calculated for the period examined: Total investor return rate and annualized investor return rate. Total return rate is determined by calculating the investor return dollars as a percentage of the net of the sales, redemptions and exchanges for each period.*

DALBAR © 2016   QUANTITATIVE ANALYSIS OF INVESTOR BEHAVIOR   5

The S&P 500 experienced an 8.19% annualized rate of return over the previous 20 years, where the average equity mutual fund investor experienced 4.67%. The disparity is even worse looking at the previous 30 years, where the S&P 500 experienced 10.35% vs the average equity mutual fund investor at 3.66%.

What if there was an investment that never experienced any losses or volatility for the entire 30 years and only averaged 5% per year compared to the S&P 500's 10.35%? At first glance it appears that investment drastically underperformed. However, when you compare the 5% per year with the actual performance of the human being of only 3.66% by letting fear and greed control the decisions along the way, it turns out this investment delivered better results than the particular investor, regardless of what the actual market did.

The magic of compounding:

Warren buffet once called compounding the "eighth wonder of the world." Once again, Warren wasn't wrong.

Let's say you had $100,000 to start, and then lost 50% your first year, and then made 50% your second year. How much do you have after the end of year two? The answer – is 75,000. Take a look at the chart below. If you lose 50%, you need 100% to get back to even.

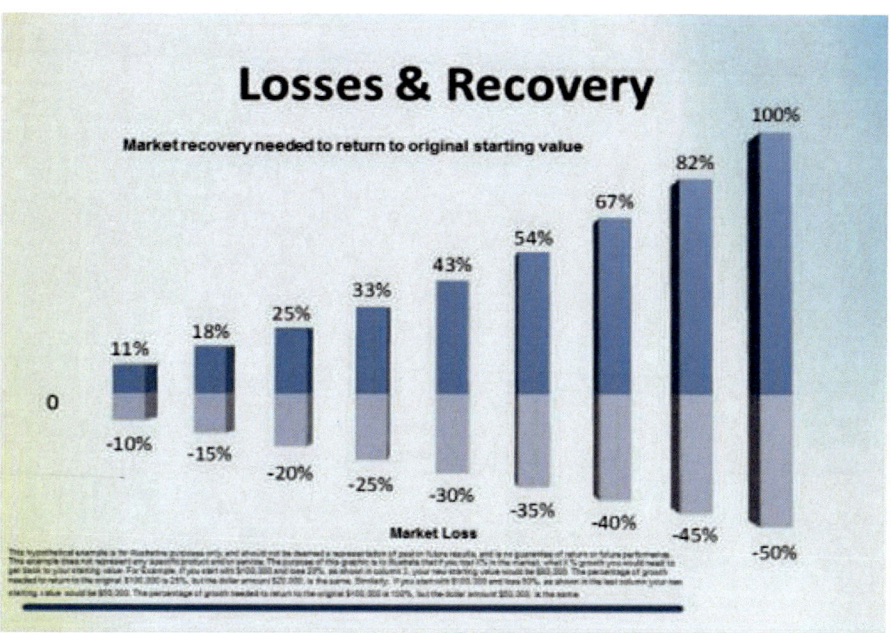

However, what is the "average annual return" of the investment itself in my example? It's simply zero. Average annual returns just take the series of returns (positive 50% year one and negative 50% year two) and divide by the amount of years.

Wouldn't it be misleading to see a mutual fund that has averaged zero percent yet you are down $25,000 dollars?

Take a look at the next example below to illustrate this point further.

	End of Year	S&P 500 Principal	Percent Gain				
actual year		$ 1,000,000		$	1,000,000		
2002	1	$ 779,000	-22.10%	$	1,000,000	-22.10%	0.00%
2003	2	$ 1,002,417	28.68%	$	1,143,400	28.68%	14.34%
2004	3	$ 1,111,480	10.88%	$	1,205,601	10.88%	5.44%
2005	4	$ 1,166,054	4.91%	$	1,235,198	4.91%	2.46%
2006	5	$ 1,350,174	15.79%	$	1,332,717	15.79%	7.90%
2007	6	$ 1,424,298	5.49%	$	1,369,300	5.49%	2.75%
2008	7	$ 897,308	-37.00%	$	1,369,300	-37.00%	0.00%
2009	8	$ 1,134,736	26.46%	$	1,550,459	26.46%	13.23%
2010	9	$ 1,305,627	15.06%	$	1,667,208	15.06%	7.53%
2011	10	$ 1,333,176	2.11%	$	1,684,798	2.11%	1.06%
2012	11	$ 1,546,484	16.00%	$	1,819,581	16.00%	8.00%
2013	12	$ 2,047,390	32.39%	$	2,114,263	32.39%	16.20%
			avg ann returns				
			8.22%				6.57%

This is for hypothetical illustrative purposes only. This is NOT indicative of an investment nor a recommendation of any kind

On the left, this is simply taking a look at the TOTAL return numbers for the S&P 500 for each calendar year from 2002 through 2013, and a one million dollars starting investment. On the right, is simply assuming you lose no money when the market goes down, but only make half of the S&P 500's return on the positive years.

Ten of the twelve years were positive, so the investor on the right would only be making half of the returns ten times out of twelve, and simply not lose money the other two years. If you look at the average annual returns, the actual market was higher at 8.22% compared to the hypothetical which shows 6.57%. However, if you look at where the one million dollar starting investment grew to on each occasion, you will see the hypothetical finished with more money. This is the magic of compounding. In 2009 as an example, the S&P 500 made 26.46% but it only made this return off of the $897,308 value after the market went down. For the hypothetical on the right, in 2009 it only made 13.23%, however it made the return off of the $1,369,300 value.

The point here is not to persuade someone to invest aggressively or conservatively. It's also not to suggest that one will do better than the other in the future. Once again, neither I nor anyone else can know that. The point is to simply understand ahead of time who you are as an investor and stay consistent. If you are someone who wants to be conservative, do not switch strategies AFTER the market has done terrific. If you are someone who wants to be aggressive, do not switch strategies AFTER the market has had a major correction.

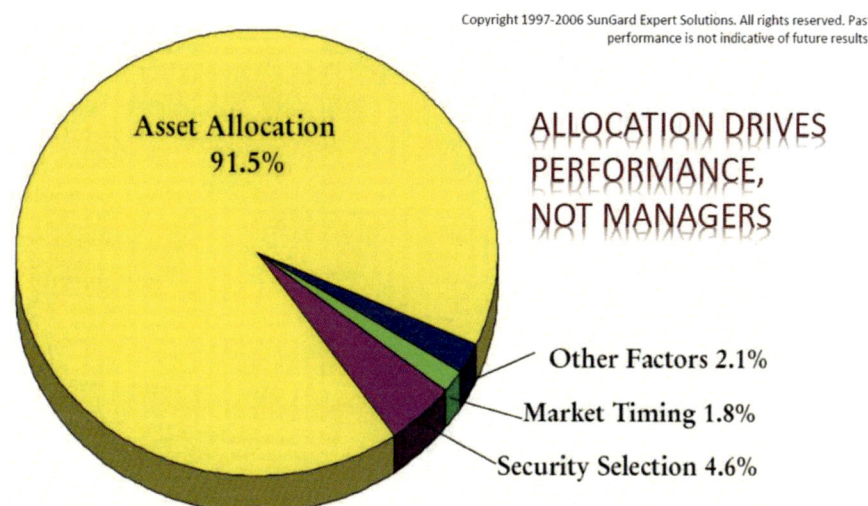

"WHO IS MAKING YOUR ASSET ALLOCATION DECISIONS FOR YOU?"

Asset Allocation:

What's the golden rule for real estate? Location, location, location! I don't have to know anything about picking houses if I end up on Rodeo Drive, the worst house probably does quite well over time compared to the best house in most neighborhoods. When building a portfolio, the biggest driver of returns, after risk tolerance, has historically been asset allocation.

Once we know the composition of the portfolio, thanks to the goals and risk tolerance analysis, we need to determine how that is properly represented. How much in stocks vs bonds? How much in domestic vs international? How much in large cap vs small cap? And the list goes on.

Stocks, Bonds, Mutual Funds, Index Funds and ETF's:

After you build out the proper asset allocation, the next step is to pick the most efficient tools that represent each asset class. As mentioned my goal is not to go into detail on specific investments with this book, however, the mutual fund is the most common investment for Americans, and I would be remiss if I didn't share insights into them.

Mutual funds were created back in the early 1900's to give investors diversification and professional management. If you placed all of your money in one single stock, you would not only have stock market risk in general, but you would have the risk that the overall market does fine and yet something horrible happens to just your one company. As you keep diversifying into other companies as well as sectors and industries within the market, you further and further reduce your risk until you end up with simply the overall stock market risk.

One stock mutual fund might have 100 different stocks inside of it. You own a little piece of this fund that you share with hundreds of thousands of other investors. You can put one hundred dollars into this one fund, and instantly own 100 different stocks. As the decades went by, mutual funds became more popular, and today there are more mutual funds than individual stocks themselves. I'm not going to generalize and claim all mutual funds are good or bad for all investors, there are simply three things I want you to be aware of when looking at mutual funds.

Fees, Flexibility, and Potential Tax Ramifications:
Fees:

Every time a stock or a bond inside of the mutual fund is bought or sold, there is a trading fee which you as the investor pay. Added to this, is the expense ratio of the fund. There are a few other costs associated, but let's stick with these two for the moment. You could be paying less than 1% per year between these two costs, or more than 3% per year between these two line items.

This was the idea behind the inception of the index fund. The idea was to simply assume a diversified stock market index like the S&P 500 hundred combined with keeping costs down could dramatically outperform funds with higher fees. The actively managed fund would make the claim that the money manager knows which stocks to pick better than the passive index, and therefore even after the fees the investor would be better off.

The mutual fund fees you pay are not transparent but are being taken out as the fund goes along. It is important to get an analysis done on what you are actually paying for the fund, and if net of the fees, it is able to provide overall value long term compared to another similar investment choice.

Flexibility:

It's important to understand how the structure of a mutual fund works. If you own a mutual fund and you want to "sell" your fund, you don't actually sell the fund to another person. You simply "redeem" your shares back to the mutual fund company. The company therefore needs to have the cash on hand, or sell investments to raise the cash to give back to you. This can be a problem for the flexibility of a mutual fund portfolio manager when market swings occur that set off the emotional buying and selling of average investors.

If a huge downturn in the market occurs, the mutual fund manager ideally would not want to sell at the bottom and make this emotional mistake – after all they are the professionals. However, as you've learned, the other hundreds of thousands of investors will want to sell. If they all want to redeem at the same time back to the fund company, then the portfolio manager would have no choice but to sell the stocks at the worst moment in order to raise the cash for all of its investors. This means the irrational behavior of the investors can handcuff the manager – and affect your money.

Taxes: Please note this part is only relevant to mutual funds you own in NON retirement accounts. Mutual funds you own inside IRA accounts will not have this issue.

Let's say one of the hundred stocks inside the mutual fund is Coca Cola, and the mutual fund bought the stock when it was trading at $80 per share. It then does well, and goes to $90 per share, which happens to be when you buy into the mutual fund. Now let's say Coca Cola takes a step backwards and drops to $85 per share, and the portfolio manager decides to sell. Your experience was a $5 per share loss. However, you will actually pay a $5 per share capital gain! The reason is because the fund bought the stock at $80 per share and it was sold at $90 per share for a gain while you were in the fund. Basically, this means in non-retirement accounts, you might unfortunately be paying other people's taxes! If nothing else, it lets you know that with mutual funds you can't control your own destiny as far as when you pay capital gains, and how much and at what time. All of the buying and selling inside the fund per year is out of your control and delivering you a 1099 whether you like it or not.

Index Funds:

An index mutual fund is one where there is no active manager picking and choosing stocks and therefore very little trading occurs which can drastically drive down the fees and tax ramifications described above.

ETF's: Exchange Traded Funds:

The invention of the exchange traded fund was designed to deliver the instant diversification that a mutual fund has, yet in a different structure ideally designed to lower the fees and tax ramifications described above.

The biggest difference between an ETF and an index fund is that an ETF still trades like a stock from one human being to another and does not get redeemed back to the mutual fund company. In other words, if I want to sell my ETF it goes to another human being who will buy that ETF, instead of redeeming back to the fund company to raise the cash to give back to the investor.

The bottom line, is we are searching for the very best tool to represent each of the asset classes we decided on when building our portfolio. We have to take all of these factors into consideration, and then determine if we feel a stock, bond, mutual fund, index fund, or ETF is the best tool to represent the specific asset class it's representing.

Overall Summary:

First, build your portfolio tailored to your goals and needs. Second, concentrate on the appropriate risk tolerance specific to your comfort level. Next, is to build the asset allocation to maximize that given portfolio we're now looking for. Finally, we then do our due diligence to determine which tool (stock, bond fund, or ETF) represents each asset class.

Annuities:

Annuities are maybe the most polarizing and confusing product for retirees. Therefore I would once again be remiss if I didn't shed some light on this type of investment.

An annuity is a contractual agreement between an insurance company and you. You can buy annuities specifically for growth, income, or death benefit reasons. However, the whole idea of an annuity is to deliver some sort of guaranteed result. There are three main worlds of annuities as I see them: Fixed, Fixed Indexed, and Variable.

A Fixed annuity is very similar to a CD. You buy a pre-determined guaranteed interest rate for a guaranteed period of years. As an example, if you buy a 5 year fixed annuity at 3%, this means you are guaranteed 3%

interest per year over the 5 years. There are typically no out of pocket fees to the investor, and there are typically penalties to pull your money out early (remember that safety and return means lack of liquidity).

The main difference is that a bank issues a CD while an insurance company issues a fixed annuity. Also, for NON-retirement accounts, even if you don't want the interest from the CD, you will still have to recognize it that year on your tax return. With the fixed annuity, you can defer the taxation until you spend the income, and it will be taxable in the year that you spend it.

On the polar opposite side of the annuity world are variable annuities. A variable annuity is typically a collection of mutual funds you choose from to build out your risk tolerance and asset allocation. Your money goes up and down based on how the mutual funds perform, no different than if you own the funds outside of the variable annuity. There is typically an insurance wrapper around the mutual funds that creates a basic guaranteed death benefit. As an example, if you deposited $100,000 into the variable annuity, and the funds do poorly and the account goes down to $80,000 and you pass away, your beneficiaries will inherit the $100,000 you put in. For this basic death benefit, there are extra fees on top of the mutual fund fees that already exist. These are typically called mortality and expense fees.

Typically the variable annuity will have a surrender schedule where you will pay penalties to move out of the variable annuity should you choose to. These can be 3 years or 10 years depending on the product you purchase.

Just like the fixed annuity, if you choose NON-retirement account dollars, the gains will grow tax deferred rather than receive a yearly 1099, which is a benefit. However, the gains become taxable later on when you want to take money out of the annuity.

Variable annuities tend to be much higher in fees, and they tend to typically lock up your money for a period of time. Yet, they don't provide you protection from the market falling anymore than the mutual funds themselves will fall. Also, they tend to pay large commissions to the brokers who sell the products, and the commissions do not show up on the statement.

As you can hopefully tell by now this book is not meant to be opinion based on which investments I personally like or dislike. With that being said, the pure facts are that most of the bad press you hear about annuities in general stems from the variable side of the annuity world for the above reasons.

The fixed indexed annuity was created to offer the guarantees associated with the fixed annuity, yet with more upside if the market does well. Because they have elements of guarantees and market upside, you might often hear them referred to as "hybrid" annuities. The idea is that you choose a market index with which to link your money. These days you have many choices from the S&P 500 index to the Dow Jones, MSCI, gold, interest rates, and many other options. Once you choose the index with which you want to be linked, there are many ways you can link your money to that index.

The entire point of the index annuity is that no matter which index you choose, and no matter which way you choose to link your money to that index, if the index goes down you are guaranteed to not lose any of your principal – no matter how much the index goes down.

Let's use an example for the S&P 500 index. We are going to look at an Annual Point to Point strategy with a cap of 6%. If you purchase this annuity on July 1, you are looking at the S&P index value on July 1 and then seeing where it finishes one year later. If the index goes down, you will not make or lose any money. If the index goes up, you will make all of what the index makes up to a maximum of 6% for the year.

You may also decide to choose an annual point to point strategy with a 50% participation strategy and no cap. This time you also link your money to the S&P 500 on a one year basis starting July 1. However, this time you will make 50% of whatever the index makes when it goes up, but with no cap on how much you can make that year. However, as always, if the index goes down you still lose nothing.

These are only two basic examples. There are plenty of index choices and even managed solutions now, and plenty more ways to link your money to these choices than the two described above.

Fixed indexed annuities typically have little or no fees on the products themselves, and as with all annuities, a commission that goes to the broker or agent who sells them. Also, as with all annuities, for the guarantees they provide you will have a period of time where you have early surrender penalties if you pull out your investment. Finally, as with other annuities, in non-retirement accounts the gains do grow tax deferred but will be taxable when you eventually take them out.

Riders:

The above describes how the different annuity products themselves work. However, you can also add optional features to the annuities known as "riders." A full description of all of the rider choices in the industry is beyond the scope of this book, but I will mention a basic option below to illustrate how they work. We will look at a "Lifetime Income rider."

A lifetime income rider is for someone looking to create a future guaranteed income stream. You can add this rider to either a variable annuity, or a fixed indexed annuity. What happens is that now you will have two values with your annuity. You will have your "accumulation value" and your "income value." The accumulation value is the money linked to the mutual funds or the index. This is the amount that you can walk away with someday if you don't want the annuity anymore. This is also the value to your beneficiaries should you pass away. The income value is simply what the income rider is growing at each year. This is NOT the value you could walk away with someday should you choose to, and NOT the inheritable value should you pass away. This is simply the value your future guaranteed income stream will be based off of when you decide to turn on your income.

The other component (and in my opinion the most important component) of the income rider, is the withdrawal percentage depending on what age you are when you choose to take your lifetime income.

One last piece of information is that a lot of annuity products will give you a day one "bonus" on products where you add the income rider. This is an incentive to get into the product, because if you add the lifetime income rider they feel you will very likely stay in the product for your entire life.

Example: Let's use a 60 year old looking to deposit $200,000 dollars into a fixed indexed annuity linked to the S&P 500 annual point to point with a 5% cap. We are also going to add the lifetime income rider to this product, which provides a 6% bonus day one, and a 7% compounded growth rate each year for the income value. The withdrawal percentage starts out at 4.25% at age 60, and gets better by 0.1% each year. See next page.

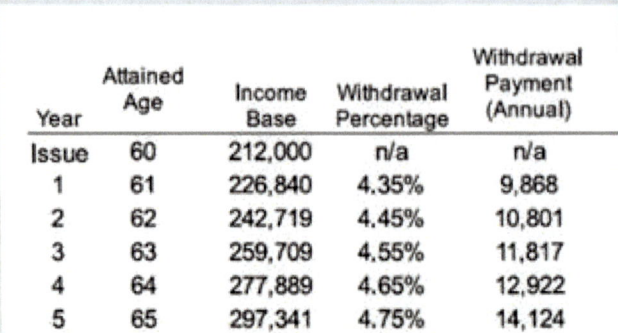

Income Value Only

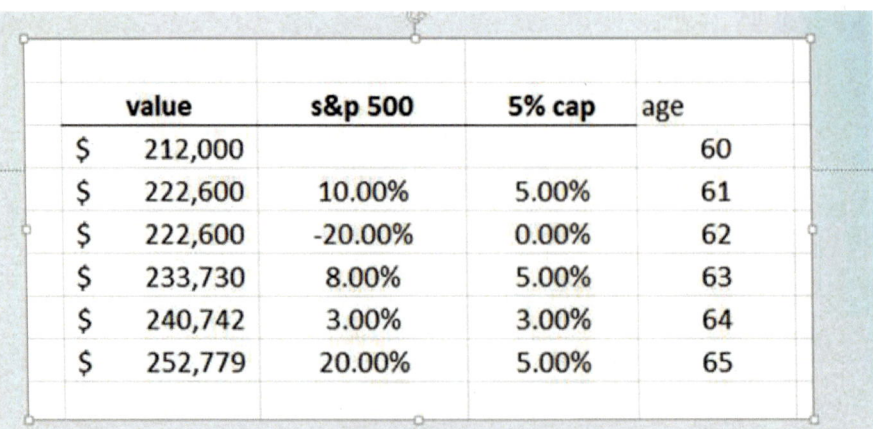

accumulation value

As you can see from the chart on the previous page the $200,000 deposit, which became $212,000, will have the income rider grow to a guaranteed value of $297,341 by age 65 and provide a 4.75% withdrawal rate equal to a guaranteed lifetime income stream of $14,124. Once you take the income, it will typically be level for life. As you take that income out each year, it will reduce the $252,779 accumulation value by that amount each year. However, the money is still linked to the S&P 500 in the annual cap strategy. This means in years where the market goes up, although you pulled out the income, you will still have some gains replenishing some or maybe all of what you took out. With that being said, inevitably the accumulation value will be going down each year. The entire point of the income rider is that if the money runs out someday, the insurance company will still pay you the income for as long as you live. This is basically setting up a personal pension for yourself, but one in which you still control the money along the way if you change your mind, and one in which the money is still fully inheritable along the way.

Consider how much less income you would be getting if you chose to put your money in something that grew at 4% per year and you took out the new prudent withdrawal percentage of 3% per year. This time your $200,000 grew to $243,331 and pulling out 3% would provide you $7,300 dollars of annual income. The income rider will now provide a guaranteed income stream of $14,124 per year – ALMOST DOUBLE! The message is that the income rider is technically this hypothetical value that you can't touch in a lump sum or provide inheritability off of. However, if your only goal is a guaranteed income stream, then it's a very real value and a very meaningful one. It also lets you pull more than the prudent man's rule of 3% and it's ok because if the money runs out someday your income still continues.

Income riders are typically what is used to fund the flooring income strategy.

Summary:

As you can see by now, annuities are incredibly complex because there are different types that act very differently from one another. Beyond that, each type of annuity has tons of different nuances and choices that act very differently from one another. Finally, there are many different forms of complex riders you can add to the products that act in very different ways and provide very different results.

If you are looking for a guaranteed result from your investment, an annuity might very well be a good choice for you. However, you need to be extremely careful in the annuity world. It is only appropriate to put a manageable amount of your overall money in them because of the lack of liquidity. Because the complexity of the product and the high commissions associated with them, they may be abused by salespeople even if it isn't in your best interest. Finally, even if it is in your best interest, there are many companies that make many different versions of these products, and it's crucial to pick the very best product that exists. Some are much worse than others, and it can turn a good idea into an expensive mistake.

Investment Summary:

Once you build your overall plan, you will understand your income and growth needs and start choosing investments based off of those needs. From there, you will diversify to achieve your safety, liquidity, and return targets. Then, you will build something tailored to your risk tolerance. Next, you will choose the individual investments tools (mutual funds, etfs, annuities etc.) that are best suited to meet those needs. Finally, you need to do the due diligence to find out which company and which products are the very best option.

CHAPTER 5

BE TAX EFFICIENT! WITH YOUR INCOME PLAN AND INVESTMENT PLAN

I cannot stress enough how important tax planning is in the context of retirement planning. During our working years, tax planning is pretty simple. The more money you make, the more taxes you pay. Each new dollar you bring in from wages adds to your taxable income for the year, taxed at higher and higher rates as your income increases. Sure, you can put money away into your 401k or IRA to get some deductions (up to IRS limits). Sure, you can write off your mortgage interest or give money to charity for extra deductions – but that's all money you have to SPEND just to get PART of that money back in the form of a deduction.

Unfortunately, far too many people and even far too many advisors only focus on the investment planning. This can cause them to lose sight of the tax implications of their decisions, and that can be very detrimental to the long term success of the retirement plan.

Retirement is the first time in your life you get to CHOOSE from where you get your income. Most people have never thought about that concept before. As you hopefully remember from the beginning of this book, the first step in all of retirement planning is to determine your NET after tax income goal. Now, we get to CHOOSE where we get that income from.

Different accounts and investments have different tax characteristics. The whole idea with tax planning in retirement is to understand how to pull income from the right combination of accounts and investments to lower the overall amount of tax you have to pay.

To understand how to do this, let's go step by step.

Tax Brackets:

First you need to have a basic understanding of how the tax system works in this country. Here is an example of 2017 tax rates for a married couple filing jointly.

2017 Federal Income Tax Tables

Filing Status	Taxable Income	Marginal Tax Bracket
Married Filing Jointly	Not over $18,650	10%
	Over $18,651 but not over $75,900	15%
	Over $75,901 but not over $153,100	25%
	Over $153,101 but not over $233,350	28%
	Over $233,351 but not over $416,700	33%
	Over $416,701 but not over $470,700	35%
	Over $470,700	39.6%

Source: www.IRS.gov
http://taxfoundation.org/article/2016-tax-brackets

Let's say you and your spouse earned a combined $120,000 dollars of income from your job in 2017 and had no other sources of income. This would put you in the 25% MARGINAL tax bracket. This simply lets you know that each additional dollar you bring home will be taxed at 25% at the federal level for the rest of the calendar year.

In this example however, the first $18,650 dollars are only taxed at 10%. All of the dollars between $18,651 and $75,900 are only taxed at 15%. It is ONLY the dollars between $75,901 and $120,000 that are taxed at 25%. Once you blend in all of the rates, your EFFECTIVE tax rate will look like this

2016 Federal Income Tax Tables

- **Marginal Tax Rate Example:**
  - Married filing joint with $120,000 per year in income:

Taxable Income	Marginal Tax Rate and amount
$0-$18,550	10% or $1,855
$18,551-$75,300	15% or $8512.35
$75,301-$120,000	25% or $11,174.75

Total tax paid= **$21,542.10** or Net Tax Rate of **18%**

This hypothetical example is for illustrative purposes only, should not be deemed a representation of past or future results and is no guarantee of return or future performance. This example does not represent any specific product and/or service.

Then from here you get to start using the standard deduction we all get, or your itemized deductions, whichever is greater- plus your personal exemptions and any other exemptions if you still claim dependents. Let's use the example where this couple simply has their standard deductions and no other dependents to claim.

	2017
Filing Status	Joint
Personal Exemptions	2
Ordinary Income	120,000
Adjusted Gross Income	120,000
Standard Deduction	12,700
Taxable Income	99,200
AMTI Net of Exemption	35,500
Schedule or Table Tax	16,278
Tentative Minimum Tax	9,230
Net Federal Tax	16,278

Actual effective rate of 13.57%

As you can now see, this couple will pay a total tax for the year of $16,278 off of the total of $120,000 of income they actually received. This means when you divide the total amount of tax they have to pay into the total amount of income they received, their true effective tax rate is actually 13.57%.

This is very helpful for a number of reasons. 1) Now you know the actual amount of tax you will pay before the year even starts. This means you will know exactly how much to withhold in taxes for the year so there aren't any bad surprises come April 15th.

However, this example was just suggesting this couple earned $120,000 combined incomes from work, which is all taxable income. Remember in retirement we will be generating the income from a number of different places, so is there a way to pay fewer taxes on $120,000 of total income?

What accounts do what?

If you're fortunate enough to have a pension, then this will be dollar for dollar ordinary taxable income (note, unless something such as a VA disability portion which could be tax free).

Think of your traditional IRA's, 401k's and retirement plans like a shell. The money you deposited into the shell gave you a tax deduction. it does not matter what investment you place inside of this shell, any earnings or interest or dividends will stay in the IRA shell tax deferred, meaning you won't pay taxes along the way. Once you go to take money out of this shell and spend it, then it becomes taxable income for the year.

Roth accounts are a different version of this shell. The initial money you deposited into the Roth did NOT give you a tax deduction at the time. Also, it does not matter what investment you place inside of this shell, any earnings or interest or dividends will stay in the ROTH shell tax deferred, meaning you won't pay taxes along the way. However this time, once you go to take money out of this shell and spend it, it will be 100% tax free and not show up as taxable income. (As long as a few basic guidelines are followed).

What is a "non-qualified" account? This is any account that does not qualify for some tax deferred or tax free treatments, like the traditional or Roth IRA's mentioned above. These are after tax dollars that you saved somewhere along the way. This could be in your checking or savings accounts, your brokerage accounts, trust accounts, etc. The initial money you invest here, known as your "cost basis" will never be taxed again if you want to spend it – its already been taxed. However, once you invest these dollars, the earnings or dividends or interest have their own tax implications depending on what the investment is.

Any interest you get from: a corporate or government bond, CD or money market, or any type of annuity, will be taxed at whatever your MARGINAL tax bracket is. This is another reason knowing your marginal bracket is important, it helps you make investment decisions on your non-qualified investments. Let's look at the same couple as before as an example.

Let's say they placed $100,000 into a corporate bond paying 4% interest, or $4,000 of interest for the year. We know they are already in the 25% marginal bracket because of their income, which means they will owe 25% tax on this interest, or $1,000 of actual tax for the year - only keeping $3,000 of the interest. (Please note this is just federal taxation, depending on your residence state tax could also apply).

What if they also had the ability to invest in a comparable municipal bond that was federally tax free paying 3.2% interest? Because there is no tax on this investment, they get to keep the entire $3,200 of interest.

Essentially, even though the corporate bond paid more interest, after taxes the municipal bond ended up being better for this couple based off of their marginal tax rate.

However, let's now pretend this same couple was only in the 15% marginal bracket because their combined income was only $60,000 for the year? This time with the corporate bond interest, they would only owe 15% in taxes, and would be able to keep $3,400 of the $4,000 of interest after tax.

That means this time it's actually better for this couple to invest in the taxable bond, because even after paying taxes they will walk away with more interest than the municipal bond that was tax free.

Knowing your marginal bracket helps us determine what is known as your "tax equivalent yield." That's a fancy way for saying "based on your own tax bracket and looking at multiple investments with different tax characteristics, after all taxes are paid, what do you get to keep the most of."

These investments that give off taxable interest are easy to memorize – your tax liability is simply your own marginal bracket.

Dividends from stocks are a bit trickier under current law. Dividends from stocks can either be classified as "ordinary dividends" or "qualified dividends." There are multiple rules that determine whether a dividend from a stock gets treated as ordinary or qualified which is outside of the scope of this book, however it's much better to be classified as qualified.

An ordinary dividend from a stock has identical treatment as the bond, CD, or annuity interest described above. It's simply your marginal tax bracket.

For qualified dividends, if you are in the 15% marginal bracket or lower, then you pay no taxes under current law. Once you are in the 25% marginal bracket or higher, you will pay 15% tax on your qualified dividends. This means no matter what your marginal bracket is, qualified dividends have a lower tax rate than your marginal bracket, and are therefore more tax friendly.

What about capital gains? If you put $100,000 into a stock and sell it for $110,000, then you have a $10,000 capital gain. If you held the stock for at least one year, this is classified as a long term capital gain. If you held the stock for less than one year, it is a short term capital gain.

Short term capital gains get treated exactly like bond/CD/annuity interest, and ordinary dividends – it's simply your marginal bracket.

Long term capital gains get the same treatment as qualified dividends – either no tax at all or 15%. See the "Taxation of Investment/Interest Income" chart below.

Taxation of Investment/Interest Income

- Interest Income
- Capital Gains
- Dividend Income

Ordinary Income Tax Rates	Long-term Capital Gain & Qualified Dividend Tax Rates
10%, 15%	0%
25%, 28%, 33%, 35%	15%
39.6%	20%

Please note that once you are in the top marginal bracket, you do actually pay 20% on qualified dividends and long term capital gains.

What about Social Security?

Social security is the trickiest of all as far as how it is taxed. Before we know how much of your social security benefit is going to end up on your tax return, there is a formula known as "provisional income" that needs to be done to determine this.

Provisional income is essentially half of all of the social security income the household brings in, plus everything else. Everything else in this case means taxable pensions, money that comes out of traditional IRA's and 401K's, taxable and tax free interest, ordinary and qualified dividends, as well as short or long term capital gains. The only thing that is NOT included in provisional income is your own cost basis of your non-qualified dollars, and all money coming out of Roth IRA's. (Note if you structure it correctly the cash value in life insurance policies can also come out tax free and will not be a part of the provisional income test). See the following chart "Getting surprised by taxes".

Getting surprised by taxes
Taxation of Social Security Benefits

Percentage of benefits that are taxable	Combined income[1] limitations for taxation of Social Security retirement benefits[2]	
	Single, head of household and qualifying widower	Married filing jointly
0%	Below $25,000	Below $32,000
Up to 50%	$25,000 - $34,000	$32,000 - $44,000
Up to 85%	Above $34,000	Above $44,000

[1] On your 1040 tax return, your combined income is the sum of your adjusted gross income, plus nontaxable interest, plus one-half of your Social Security benefits.
[2] If you are married filing separately or your spouse is making deductible contributions to a retirement plan, special taxation rules may apply.
Source: Social Security Administration- https://www.ssa.gov/planners/taxes.html

This doesn't mean your social security benefits are taxed at 50% or 85%, it simply means 50% of the social security benefits you receive end up as taxable income on your return, or 85%, or none at all.

One question I am asked is "what happens if your provisional income is $31,999 vs. $32,000 even?" Does this mean your social security dollars go from non-taxed to 50% of the benefits being on your return immediately? The answer is no. As you cross these thresholds your social security starts to scale up to where as much as 50% can end up on the return, or as much as 85% can end up on your return. Please note the formula is more complex than simply what you are seeing, however it is beyond the scope of this book.

Let's take a look at another example of a tax return similar to before. Here we will assume this couple has a pension of $21,180 and $38,412 of combined social security benefits. Now they are looking to pull out $50,000 dollars and are trying to decide if they should pull it from their traditional IRA's or their non-qualified dollars sitting in their bank accounts. We will compare the impact on the overall return side by side.

	Case 1	Case 2
Income:		
Social Security Benefits	4,193	32,650
Other Income	21,180	71,180
Total Income	25,373	103,830
Total Adjustments	0	0
Adjusted Gross Income	25,373	103,830
Personal Exemptions	8,100	8,100
Total Itemized	0	0
Standard Deduction	12,700	12,700
Total Deductions from AGI	20,800	20,800
Taxable Income	4,573	83,030
Regular Tax:		
Schedule or Table Tax	457	12,235
Appropriate Regular Tax	457	12,235
Total Federal Taxes	457	12,235
Net Federal Tax Due	457	12,235

Case 1 is showing the $50,000 coming from the non-qualified bank account money, case 2 is showing it coming from a traditional IRA. In case 1, you will notice how the bank money does not show up on a return anywhere. Also, it keeps the provisional income low to where only $4,193 of the $38,412 social security dollars ended up taxable. This couple simply uses their personal exemptions and standard deductions once again, and the total federal tax for the year is now only $457!

In case 2 you will now see $71,180 as the total "other income." This is because the $50,000 from a traditional IRA is all added as income for the year. However, it also increases their provisional income and causes 85% of the social security dollars to now be taxable. With all else being equal now they will owe $12,235 dollars of federal taxation.

> Basically, the $50,000 coming out of the IRA caused an extra $11,778 in taxes!

Each new dollar you take out of an IRA could cause your social security to also retroactively end up on your return. This could push your whole bracket to go from let's say the 15% marginal bracket to the 25% bracket. This means that you would be paying more tax on that IRA withdrawal than you thought. It also means you would be paying more tax on the corporate bond or the CD than you thought. This also means all of your qualified dividends and capital gains went from nontaxable, to taxable at 15%.

Can you see how there is a domino effect when it comes to tax planning in retirement?

Tying the Whole Thing Together:

Unfortunately, most people will simply start pulling money from their accounts once they get into retirement and after the year is over simply pay whatever tax their CPA says they owe. Once we have gone through the first two steps in this book, we want to truly understand the most tax efficient way to fund your gap. If you can pull money from the right accounts and right investments, you can potentially lower your effective tax rate. Think about the ongoing implications of this. If you can lower your effective tax rate each year by this type of planning, you pay fewer taxes. If you pay fewer taxes, you don't need to pull as much money out of your accounts to end up at your net income goal. If more money gets to stay invested in your accounts, then it gets to continue to earn a compounded rate of return over your retirement years. I have personally seen plans where if you can lower your effective rate each year by 5% because of proper planning, it adds hundreds of thousands of dollars to my clients ending plan balance.

Now you are truly seeing why step number one in this entire process is understanding your AFTER tax net income goal.

CHAPTER 6
Protect Your Retirement Income Plan Through a Proper Health care coverage, Long Term Care, and Estate Plan

This book has walked you through the step by step process of how you build your retirement income plan. Making sure you have a good income stream for life is the name of the game and is what creates the comfortable retirement for which we're all searching. The engine that runs that plan is the proper investment and tax strategies you have seen. However, even a well-built retirement plan can come crumbling down if you don't protect it. The topics of insurance planning and estate planning are comprehensive in nature and would require an entire book in and of itself.

As an example, there are many insurance products designed specifically to be investments and grow your money tax free for use in retirement. Also, there are other insurance products simply designed to provide the best legacy benefit should that be your goal. The insurance discussion we will be having is strictly centered on protecting your retirement plan should a health event occur.

My purpose is to help you understand the key elements to consider and plan for. As always, I urge you to consult with a personal financial planner to discuss the details of your specific situation.

Long Term Care Planning:

Most of your health care planning will be covered through your normal health insurance in retirement. For many people this will involve Medicare part A and Part B. This covers all of your inpatient and outpatient coverage, doctors' visits, medication, etc. Many others will also look into buying a supplemental insurance to help with any gaps Medicare part A and B may not cover.

The real concern, and an ever increasing one statistically, is what happens should you ever have a long term care event – which is NOT something covered by any form of health insurance mentioned above.

A long term care event is defined in one of two ways. The first, is your inability to do two of the six activities of daily living, which includes eating, dressing, bathing, toileting, transferring, and continence. Should your personal physician diagnose you with the inability to perform at least two of these, you officially have a long term care event. The second is, even if you can do all six of these, a cognitive impairment such as Alzheimer's or dementia.

Having an event like this occur likely means that you would need comprehensive care for an extended period of time, either at a facility or having care in-home. Once again this kind of care is NOT covered by any form of your health insurance, and therefore the ongoing costs can be devastating if not considered.

How likely is this to happen to me?

There are certain factors that are specific to each person's situation, such as family history and the way you have taken care of yourself throughout your life. Another is obviously, the older you are the more likely you are to need care. It is also worth noting that women are more likely statistically to need care then men are.

The concept of long term care is still relatively new and therefore we are still learning more about the statistics over time. With that being said,

Genworth's 2015 study determined 70% of people age 65 or older will require some form of long term care services and support during their lives.

How much would this kind of care cost?

The amount of money it might cost differs depending on the nature of your event, the expected amount of time for it to continue, the type of care required, and the state and city in which you live.

As an example, you may have an event that requires you to have comprehensive around the clock care. This would, of course, be more expensive than if you had an event that simply requires some care for part of the day.

We all realize that we have to pay more to stay at a five star resort than we would for the local motel. While this is a bit of a crude analogy, it illustrates the point that you have the choice of the type of care, the type of facility and these dictate the cost.

In Genworth's same 2015 study they showed that the national median hourly rate for homemaker services were $20 per hour, and adult day health care was $69 per hour. The national median daily rate for an assisted living facility was $120 per day, where a semi private room in a nursing facility was $220 per day and a private room $250 per day.

It's also important to remember that whatever the cost today, it will be increasing each year. Medical and long term care costs tend to increase even faster than the pace of general inflation.

Do I need Long Term Care Insurance?

The first thing to do is to make a prediction of how much money you think it might cost given all of the factors above. As an example, let's say you want to plan on a semi private room which today costs $6,600 a month. If you are 65 years old, you may plan around the assumption of twenty years in the future, which means it would cost $15,000 a month by then.

Next, is taking a look at the retirement plan that you've built already, and what kind of income your plan is already capable of at your age 85. Remember, when you built your initial budget which is step 1 of the entire book, you ideally included discretionary income to cover all of the fun things you want to do like hobbies and vacations. The unfortunate reality is that if you have a long term care event, you won't be doing those things anymore, and therefore the income you earmarked will now be redirected to help pay for this cost of care.

Let's say at age 85, your retirement plan was projected to provide $12,000 a month. This means you certainly wouldn't want to buy a long term care policy for $15,000 a month which is your cost of care. This means you would want to buy a long term care policy for $3,000 a month, to stack on top of the other $12,000 a month your plan is already providing, which now combined pays for the cost of care. This helps you control the cost of the long term care insurance you buy and stay within your budget, yet plan for the costs long term at the same time.

If unfortunately you do not have much in the way of assets in retirement, you will eventually be entitled to Medicaid and your state will pay for the cost of care should you be impoverished. Therefore, you most likely wouldn't want to buy long term care insurance as you really don't have any assets you are trying to protect from being spent down. Additionally, let's say you have been a tremendous saver and have millions of dollars in assets, of which could easily provide the income you need without ever dipping into your principal should you need care. You also most likely wouldn't want to buy long term care insurance as you can pay for the cost easily and sustainably. Long term care insurance is typically for people who have somewhere between a couple hundred thousand in assets to a couple million or so. This is typically where you would have to rapidly spend down your principal to pay for the care and therefore the insurance would help you avoid that and be meaningful to you.

Assessing your legacy goals are also important in this discussion. If you have no legacy goals you may avoid getting long term care insurance because you don't care about rapidly spending down your assets. However, if you do have strong legacy goals you may consider purchasing this insurance so that you avoid spending them down.

Another consideration is your primary residence if you have a lot of equity, or at least if you will have a lot of equity in the future. For some, you can consider a reverse mortgage or simply selling your property and use the equity to be your long term care plan, and therefore avoid buying any insurance.

If I do want Long Term Care Insurance, What are my Options?

There are a few forms of long term care insurance you have the option to purchase. The first one being what I would call traditional long term care insurance.

With traditional long term care insurance you purchase a daily benefit amount first, let's say $150 per day. Then you choose an elimination period, let's say 90 days. Next, you choose a term period, let's say for four years. Finally, you choose an inflation clause (always purchase at least some form of an inflation clause), let's say 5% compounded. There are other specific features you can add to your policy, but these are the main clauses you are looking for.

The example above means that once you have triggered your long term care event, the insurance won't start paying you until after the 90 day elimination period. After 90 days, it will start to pay you up to $150 a day to pay for your care. If you use all $150 every day, your benefit will last for four years. While the benefit would pay $150 per day right now, each year that amount will grow by 5% compounded to keep up with rising medical costs so that in the future it is an appropriate amount for your cost of care.

All of those options, along with your age and health rating, will dictate how much this insurance will cost. You pay your premiums each month (or quarter or year) and your insurance will stay intact. Should you be fortunate enough to never need the insurance and pass away peacefully in your sleep someday, there is typically no benefit that will come to you. Another way of saying that is the insurance company won that bet. This doesn't mean this is a bad idea, I don't wish to get in a car accident just so I feel it was worth it to pay those premiums do I? With that being said, this is one big deterrent to why people might not purchase this kind of insurance. Because of this, the insurance industry has created other forms.

Note, with traditional long term care insurance, they typically have the right to increase your premium should the company ever be in financial trouble and they can prove that to their state insurance commissioner. In fact, this has happened many times in this industry already. This has been another deterrent to purchasing this type of insurance.

The second form of insurance comes on a life insurance chasse. Here you might buy a Guaranteed Universal Life insurance for $250,000 with a 4% long term care rider attached. This means you bought a guaranteed permanent $250,000 life insurance policy. Once again the size of the insurance you buy, along with your age and health, will dictate the price. Like any other life insurance policy, at any point should you pass away, your named beneficiary will receive a $250,000 tax free check. However, should you ever need long term care, you would be able to start receiving as much as 4%, or $10,000, of the death benefit on a monthly basis tax-free to pay for your care. If you were receiving all $10,000 each month, then this would last for up to 25 months. If you started receiving $10,000 and continued for 5 months and then passed away, your beneficiary would receive the remaining $200,000 as the death benefit.

The point of this form of insurance was so the consumer would know that for the premiums they pay, one way or another a benefit will be delivered. It will either cover their long term care which is the original reason in the first place, or at least go to their beneficiary should they never need it. This avoids the feeling of the insurance company winning the bet, so to speak.

On an additional note, you can purchase this on a number of different life insurance chasses. I just described a guaranteed universal life insurance policy. This means the premiums you pay would be guaranteed to never rise, much different than the traditional form of long term care insurance and more reassuring. However, you can purchase this long term care rider on non-guaranteed universal, indexed universal, or variable universal life insurance products. You need to be extra careful here as to the continued health of the policy long term.

The third is on an annuity chasse. Remember that discussion on the lifetime income rider? Depending on your state and the individual product, some of those annuity riders will double the income for no additional cost should you ever trigger a long term care event? Typically they will double this payment for a period of let's say 5 years. If you still need care beyond that, it will revert to the original guaranteed lifetime payment for the rest of your life. This strategy is typically not enough to cover the care itself, but certainly is a nice additional free feature of a product you were already going to purchase for your retirement income plan.

Estate Planning:

For the purposes of this book this will be a brief conversation. The main discussion here is simply making sure you have all of your accounts and beneficiaries titled correctly, and your proper wills and/or trusts in order. I am not an estate planning attorney and this certainly does not constitute legal advice, below is simply a couple basic points to consider and make sure you consult your own attorney about.

If you do not have a will or trust, then the state in which you live has a plan for you instead. They will divide your assets and send them to family members of yours, which is state dependent on their systems for how they determine who gets what – and it may not be the person or persons you would have preferred. Also, you can surely bet that the attorneys and courts are going to be getting a good share of your estate in this process.

Having at least a basic Will allows you to spell out where, and to whom, your assets go when you pass. This at least ensures that all of your life's hard earned dollars goes where you want it to. However, it is important to know that a will still goes through the probate court system. Once again this depends on your state of residence and your situation as to how much, but unfortunately the probate court system and the attorneys are going to get a piece of your estate.

You also may consider forming your own living trust. A trust is a private entity, typically one in which you are the grantor (person who creates it), trustee of (person who legally makes the decisions), and beneficiary of (person who is entitled to the benefits of any assets placed in the trust). It's pretty simple, if you title your home or non-retirement assets to where the trust owns it, and then you pass away, you will avoid probate. The trust will list off who gets what just like a Will, but it does not go through the probate system. This could save your beneficiaries time, energy and frustration, and a lot of money avoiding attorney's fees and court fees.

It's important to note that your retirement accounts such as IRA's or Roth IRA's cannot be owned by your trust, they can only be individually owned by you. However, if you put a named beneficiary down on your retirement accounts these will pass to them and avoid probate even if you don't have a will or trust. Therefore, it is also very important to review how you have listed your beneficiaries on your retirement accounts.

Finally, it is important to have the proper durable powers of attorney for medical and financial situations should you become incapacitated.

There are many factors to why you consider a Will, a Trust, both or neither. There are also certain accounts you may title for your trust to own, and others where a trust would not be the owner. There are reasons to have different documents for powers of attorney and which specific documents you would have. Again, please consult your estate planning attorney.

CHAPTER 7
Summary

As you can see there is a TON to know about retirement planning beyond just specifically "what stock or mutual fund you should buy." First we have to understand how to optimize each of the steps we have talked about. It's important to truly understand social security and pensions so that you can make the best decisions here and optimize them. It's important to understand how taxes work so you can stay in the optimal brackets each year, as well as choose the correct investments from a tax standpoint. It's important to understand your investment options so you can manage your income needs, growth needs, liquidity needs, and manage your risk while getting a rate of return that will make your plan sustainable. It's certainly important to understand how to protect the plan you build with a proper health, long term care, and estate plan.

However one of the biggest messages I want you to walk away with is the need for a comprehensive plan that will cohesively put all of the above pieces and steps together for YOUR custom situation. It is impossible to choose social security correctly if you don't understand your income needs, tax situation, and investments. You will end up being tax inefficient if you don't understand which investments you have and in which accounts you have them. The list goes on.

That is why this book is a step by step guide for how to build a comprehensive and cohesive plan that can truly put all of those different pieces together for you. If you follow these steps you will be well on your way to building a successful retirement plan. With that being said, most people still certainly need some help. You might understand your taxes much better now and what you're looking to accomplish, but I still recommend working with a qualified tax professional to make sure things are executed correctly. You may understand what characteristics of investments you are now looking for, but I still recommend you seek an investment professional to help you choose the specific investment best suited to execute your plan.

Retirement is a scary endeavor for most people, but it doesn't have to be. Follow these 6 key steps to build the structure of your plan, and speak to a qualified professional to help you implement and execute the specific steps and you might be amazed at the sense of relief you will gain.

My life's mission is to help you Retire Right. My hope is this book will help set you on that path. If there is anything further that myself or my firm can do to help you implement or execute these steps please let us know and it would be our honor and privilege to serve you.

ABOUT THE AUTHOR

Bradley R. White is a Certified Financial Planner, an Investment Advisor Representative, and Vice President of Epstein & White Retirement Income Solutions, LLC. He also serves as a National Social Security Advisor.

Bradley White has made numerous television appearances on local networks, Fox News, and CBS. He's also been featured on *The Big Biz Radio Show*, with Dave Sully, and is a cohost of the weekend Radio and TV shows "*Retire Right with Epstein and White*". A graduate of San Diego State University, Bradley White has a bachelor's degree in finance.

Made in the USA
San Bernardino, CA
05 January 2018